Glitter & fall

Also by Di Brandt

Agnes in the Sky

Jerusalem, beloved

questions i asked my mother

Walking to Mojácar
with French and Spanish translations
by Charles Leblanc and Ari Belathar

Glitter & fall

Laozi's, *Dao De Jing*
trans*inha*lations

Di Brandt

TURNSTONE PRESS

Glitter & fall
copyright ©Di Brandt 2018

Turnstone Press
Artspace Building, 206-100 Arthur Street
Winnipeg, MB, R3B 1H3 Canada
www.TurnstonePress.com

Turnstone Press gratefully acknowledges the assistance of the Canada Council
for the Arts, the Manitoba Arts Council, the Government of Canada, and the
Province of Manitoba through the Book Publishing Tax Credit and the Book
Publisher Marketing Assistance Program.

Cover photograph: beach-ocean-sand-1004592 by Oleksandr Pidvalnyi from Pexels

Li Bai (Li Bo), 711 C.E. (trans. Suzanne E. Cahill)
*Transcendence and Divine Passion: The Queen Mother of the West in Medieval
China* By Cahill, Suzanne
Copyright (c) 1993 by the Board of Trustees of the Leland Stanford Jr. University. All
rights reserved. Used by permission of the publisher, Stanford University Press,
sup.org

Excerpt by Louise Halfe, from the collection from Blue Marrow, published by
Coteau Books, Regina, Canada. Used by permission of the publisher.

Printed and bound in Canada by Friesens.

Library and Archives Canada Cataloguing in Publication

Brandt, Di, author
    Glitter & fall : Laozi's, Dao De Jing transinhalations / Di Brandt.

Poems.
Issued in print and electronic formats.
ISBN 978-0-88801-645-4 (softcover).--ISBN 978-0-88801-646-1 (EPUB).--
ISBN 978-0-88801-647-8 (Kindle).--ISBN 978-0-88801-648-5 (PDF)

    I. Title. II. Title: Glitter and fall.

PS8553.R2953G55 2018   C811'54   C2018-904311-3
                                        C2018-904312-1

MANITOBA ARTS COUNCIL
CONSEIL DES ARTS DU MANITOBA

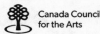
Canada Council   Conseil des arts
for the Arts   du Canada

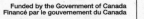
Funded by the Government of Canada
Financé par le gouvernement du Canada

Canada

Manitoba

for
Malaya, Autumn, Geordana, Rosealie,
Serenity, Cherise, Trayson, Kingston, and Sterling

At pure dawn she sounds the Celestial Drum;
A whirlwind arising, she soars upward on paired Dragons.
She plays with lightning, without resting her hands,
Traverses the clouds, without leaving a trace.
Whenever she enters the Minor Apartment Peak,
The Queen Mother will certainly be there to meet her.

—Li Bai (Li Bo), trans. Suzanne E. Cahill

How that we be brought again by the Motherhood of
Mercy and Grace into our Nature's place, where that we
were made by the Motherhood of Nature-Love: which
kindly-love, it never leaveth us. / Our Kind Mother, our
Gracious Mother, for that [God] would all wholly become
our Mother in all things…. The sweet, gracious hands of
our Mother be ready and diligently about us. For [God] in
all this working useth the office of a kind nurse that hath
nought else to do but to give heed about the salvation of
her child.

—Julian of Norwich, *Revelations of Divine Love*

She came in a Vision, flipped many faces.
Stone-aged wrinkled, creased like a stretched drum,
thin flesh, sharp nose.
When the Sun sleeps she takes faded rays,
dresses her gown. She's the burnt rose of autumn,
a blue-winged warbler. The awakened river
flanked in every woman, rolling pebbles
over and over till stone eggs are left.

—Louise Bernice Halfe, *Blue Marrow*

Table of Contents

The *Dao De Jing* is said to be the second most translated book in the world, next to the Bible. Innumerable translations and commentaries, traversing the globe and interacting dialogically with other cultures and traditions, have made of Laozi's text something more, or other, than the venerated sacred text of the Daoist religion and spiritual practice, though it is that too, in the first and foremost instance. In its diverse intercultural reception and extensive influence on artistic and intellectual practices everywhere, the *Dao De Jing* has also become a major text of the world. In the West, Laozi's presence can be seen in the work and legacy of Carl Jung, Martin Heidegger, William Carlos Williams, HD (Hilda Doolittle), Allen Ginsberg, and Mary Oliver, among many others. In Canada, poets as diverse in their poetics and affiliations as Gary Geddes, Fred Wah, Larissa Lai, and Joanne Arnott reflect Daoist presence in their writing.

I have ventured, with a certain temerity, to join this illustrious company, offering these Canadian prairie-inflected poetic meditations and creative re-translations to the existing oeuvre of Laozi's poems in English, presented in somewhat random, partial, intuitive order and fashion. I call the poems trans*inha*lations, a term coined by Montreal-based novelist and translator Robert Majzels to describe creative engagements with ancient texts. Great texts lend themselves to each historical and cultural moment and speak to it anew. In this moment, in my own place and time, a striking aspect of the *Dao De Jing* is its veneration of the feminine and maternal, as gestalt and attitude, and enduring generative principle of creation and reproduction. The great nameless Dao becomes the Grand Womb of the Cosmos, bringing forth the "ten thousand creatures." Though She is Feminine in nature, the Great Mother initiates and animates the whole Dance of Life and therefore precedes (and exceeds) the polarities of *yin* and *yang*, female and male, dark and light, day and night, which animate the creation of life and movement on earth. (French theorist Luce Irigaray calls this pre-polarized feminine principle "placental" in the human context, noting that the maternal womb and breasts nourish male and female embryos and infants alike.)

In the Daoist tradition, the Divine Feminine is associated with cosmic and earthly right governance, and known as the exalted Queen Mother of the West, and the Greatly Numinous and Ninefold Radiant Mother of Metal of Tortoise Terrace, among other extravagant Names. In the ancient Mediterranean tradition, She was known variously as Ishtar, Asherah, and Inanna, or more generically, the Queen of Heaven. The Roman Catholic Church retained some of Her pre-Christian powers in the veneration of the Virgin Mary, Mother of God, the Madonna, and Mary, Queen of Heaven—though She has been more associated with ideas of forgiveness and blessing in this tradition than governing leader. In First Nations mythology and the religious traditions of Turtle Island, She is revered as Spider Grandmother, Creatix of All That Is, as Xmucané, Grandmother of the Light, as Sky Woman, as

Changing Woman, and in many other powerful guises. She appears to the devout as White Buffalo Woman, Yellow Corn Woman, and other human-seeming forms, to bring teachings of right action in ritual and social relations. In these and other ways, She retains Her ancient primacy in areas of governance and the spiritual, physical, and psychic transformation of human life on this planet. According to Keres poet and knowledge keeper Paula Gunn Allen, the colonization of the Americas by the Spanish conquistadors was more about the suppression of matriarchy than about race. Recuperating images of the Great Mother in our present cosmologies is therefore deeply connected to restitution and the re-empowerment of Indigenous peoples, and all who have been deprived of the images and power of the Divine Feminine in the turbulent history of our era.

Another notable aspect of the *Dao De Jing*, from my intercultural vantage point, is the array of ancient Chinese institutions, figures, and landscapes in the poems, a sense of local colour which is often lost in translation, particularly in those versions which homogenize Daoist precepts for easy transport to other landscapes and time periods. I have highlighted these two aspects in my trans*inha*lations of Laozi's poems: the Great Grand-Maternal and Queenly Divine Feminine, and the sense of locality, here lightly transported to my own locale on the (multicultural and inter-cultural) Canadian prairies. I call most of the human figures in the poems women—because I am a woman, and think and write as a woman, and because women are perpetually underrepresented in public discourses on spirituality, aesthetics, and the social good (don't you agree?).

Just as women have been invited to read many import-
ant texts by and about men in diverse situations as rel-
evant to all humans, men (and those identifying other-
wise than exclusively man or woman) are invited to read
these poems as relevant also to them, and to everyone. As
Adrienne Rich observed, we are all "of woman born." We
all bear the gracious mark of the Divine Feminine, Great
Grand-Maternal, and the Heavenly Queenly in the very
fabric of our being, and all owe the Feminine in us, next to
us, and all around us, respect and care.

Laozi's poems repeatedly point to the *Nothing* that pre-
ceded the creation of All That Is, as closely preceding, if
not synonymous with, the great Cosmic Mother, though
the Poet is reluctant to give Her a single or fixed Name,
or to render Her aspect as too close to the human. This
is not, as I understand, because the Poet is shy about Her
Femininity or Maternal generativity and Queenly nurtur-
ance (and other resemblances to the human), but rather
to preserve Her grand Unnameability, Her much larger
than human and even Cosmic Ineffability. It is a gesture
that preserves our imaginative freedom, allowing us to us
reflect, each in ourselves, on the inadequate and perpetu-
ally interchangeable, renewable metaphors of the Divine,
and of the Divine in us. The very flimsiness and inade-
quacy of the metaphors, the *Dao De Jing* insists, is part of
their Ineffable power, and can direct us effectively back
to a palpable, unmediated connection with the original
Great Harmony, the great creative *Nothing*, the Whole.

Such action is rarely accomplished or even aspired to in
modern life, and is quickly dismissed by those firmly wed-
ded to the complex intellectualisms of the postmodern—or

indeed to the particular archive of customs and ceremonies developed over time in any given religious tradition. And yet, the *Dao De Jing* offers us this idea, this possibility, this hope, in language that engages directly with the challenges of our time as well as Laozi's, and it is the Poet's gift to be able to do so without the paraphernalia of dogma or ritual. Little is required to understand the simple precepts of the Dao, Laozi's poems suggest, except the willingness and commitment to do so, as we rise to the (nevertheless rigorous and formidable) challenge of cultivating inner strength, gentleness, and the capacity for stillness, which can lead to inner radiance, and receptivity to the Divine. Strikingly absent in Laozi's text in its religious aspect, to Western ears, are notions of sacrifice, prohibition, substitution, shame, blame, forgiveness, and resurrection, so prominent in Abrahamic (and also ancient Greek and Roman, and to some extent, prevailing Indigenous) beliefs and practices. In its simple subtractive logic, the *Dao De Jing* more closely resembles Buddhist, Sufi, and other mystically inclined spiritual teachings and practices, though many of Laozi's teachings also resemble the parables and Beatitudes of Jesus in the New Testament in their cheerful belief in the transformative power of simplicity, and the cultivation of hope.

This is not to deny or overlook the elaborate, colourful, and extraordinary tradition of Daoist ceremony, belief, and practice that developed in China in the centuries following Laozi's lifetime, a formidable, inspiring tradition and spiritual practice well kept and written about elsewhere, whose depth and richness I can only appreciate in glimpses. Nevertheless, it is the ordinary, quiet, humane qualities of gentleness, simplicity, humility and generosity, Laozi's poems claim, that carry in themselves the immense power of transforming the troubled world and universe, able to reconnect us all to the originary Great Harmony. The process of acquiring such transformative wisdom begins with ourselves, spreading from there into the relations around us, and so to the rest of the world, and the whole omniverse. The postmodern distinctions between spirituality, social ethics, science, philosophy, and art, or for that matter, between the personal and political, do not apply. (Imagine if everyone had followed Laozi's advice instead of Machiavelli's in the development of modern social and institutional practices—what a different world we'd be living in now!)

I am told that scholars of the *Dao De Jing* often undergo mystical experiences. I, too, encountered ecstatic moments filled with light and conversely, a sort of luminous darkness, accompanied by exquisite musical sounds, as well as receiving visionary insights into the nature of being and the "meaning" of my own life. The strangeness, sheer surprise, and often contrary (even laughable!) otherworldly logic of Laozi's poems made it possible for me to bypass certain inherited resistances to poetic-spiritual engagement and, in the way of all good travel and happy meeting of strangers and aesthetic differences, I was altered and transformed by these encounters and returned to my own hybrid religious and cultural heritage, and aesthetic-spiritual practice and understanding, enriched by the experience. I was delighted and astonished, in the process, to discover the strong legacy of medieval Chinese Daoist women mystics, whose visionary lives and poetic expressions eloquently elaborated the contours of Divine Feminine presence and inspiration in their lives and in the world. I imagine my reading of the *Dao De Jing* has been influenced by the poetic and spiritual legacy of these women mystics more immediately than can be demonstrated.

Some people disapprove of creative trans*inha*lation of ancient poetic and religious traditions and texts, fearing distortions or dilutions of their original power. Many contemporary intellectuals disavow an inherent connection between poetic and spiritual impulses and traditions, preferring a stylish, mostly ironic, model of avant-garde separation between the two. For me, however, having grown up in a traditionalist religious (Plautdietsch and German-speaking Dutch Mennonite) immigrant community steeped in old forms of poetry and then schooled in modern English literature, and well-practiced in juggling different cultural paradigms, sensibilities, and languages from a young age, such intertextual and dialogic engagement—if practiced with reverence and imagination—seems natural and perhaps even essential to the psychological, social, and political challenges facing us on the local and global scale today. At the same time, I wish to affirm the careful and rigorous keeping of ancient texts, traditions, and genealogies beyond their comprehensibility or applicability to our particular intercultural moment. I am not interested in a parodic dilution of traditionalist archives or reduction of their ancient powers to contemporary mainstream—or radically hybridized understandings or communities, nor do I wish to contribute to a loss of their rich meanings in other times and places.

I understand myself to be a humble visitor, outsider, to a gorgeous, inspiring text and its complex surround, and cautious contributor to a growing intercultural appreciation of its worth around the world.

Is it possible to recuperate grand, simple notions like Beauty, *Nothing*, Wisdom and Harmony—and politically charged images of Divine Feminine veneration like the Great Mother and Queen of Heaven—and make them believable, and receivable, to our tradition-rejecting modern ears and eyes? Is it even possible, in our busy action-oriented, noisy world, to recover the transformative dynamics of *reverence* and simplicity, stillness and awe? These poetic trans*inha*lations from Laozi's *Dao De Jing* wager *Yes!* against the loud reverberation of irony and skepticism all around—keeping in mind that Laozi's recipe for wholeness sounded equally preposterous to the sophisticated populace of his time. Intense commitment is required, in other words, to the subtraction and relaxation of our habitual psychic and social practices (of worry, denial and distracting entertainment), to arrive at the simplicity and wonder—and light-hearted good humour—of Laozi's envisioned reconnection to the Great Whole.

Almost certainly intercultural engagements risk misinterpretation and misunderstanding, but possibly offer also something new, that is of value. As fierce a critic of intercultural interpretations of Daoism as Louis Komjathy concedes that if we follow the Daoist precept to become "inwardly still and outwardly reverent," visitors may "find entrance into the Daoist tradition" and discover "unexpected openings, hidden courtyards, and inner altars" there (*Daoism: A Guide for the Perplexed* 224).It has been so for me, and I am deeply grateful for the privilege of sharing these partial, approximate, hesitant, stammering intercultural poetic-spiritual reflections, whose source and wisdom and ongoing legacy is much, much larger and deeper than my own, with you. *Xiè, xie.*

Glitter & fall

Wild rose petals

Her heart was a noisy playground,
eager children chirping like seagulls.
All summer they clambered up the ladders
and slid down the iron slides of her heart.
Every evening she counted them,
craftily, clucking like a broody hen.
Eventually she forgot their names,
there were so many of them,
swinging upside down on the monkey bars,
the sons and daughters grown up,
in shirts and ties, hats and high heels.
Settling herself dreamily in her
downy empty nest, she seemed dazed,
a trimmed midsummer red willow pole,
humming in her carved rocking chair,
nuzzled by wasps, sung to by drying leaves.

Ishtar, fish star

Before space, before earth, before time,
before water, fire, air,
before trees, before seeing, before sound,
You were there, Spider Grandmother,
grizzly-tongued Oma, gorgeous
sweet-lipped, wrinkled Queen of Heaven.

You were Everything, You were *Nothing*,
You were Light, You were Dark.
You sang the Song that sang us,
You wove the Web that held us,
the Womb that expelled us
into chlorophyll and clay.
You vanished into the Moon-silvered
shadows guarding Your golden hiding place
in the fluttering Angel-covered Ark.

You glitter in the sand. You shimmer
in the hills. You gleam in the scales
of the shining perch, the magic pickerel.
You decorate the earth with amber,
tiger lilies, rosehips, granite, metal,
eagles, ants, snowbirds, fire, ice.
Your exquisite Dance of Veils.

You breathe us out and in,
holding our hand tightly as we
swim through the bottleneck
of our shrunken desires, our human
wails, back into the Grandeur of
Your Paradise, Your Garden,
Your Galaxy-studded Mountain trails.

Rough tongue

She was there before you, before everything.
She will be there long after you.
She longs after you.
She, the Great Mother, gave birth
to Heaven and Earth.
See! Even now She cradles you in Her starry arms.
She kneads you with Her silken paws,
licks you with Her rough tongue,
Her Cougar-scented Breath.

Highbush cranberry

You stride through the city like a queen.
Your silver wolf coat, earned in recent dark days,
sways above your shapely ankles.
Presidents hesitate over their coffees
in their silver towers.
The rivers may flood their banks again in spring.
The libraries are giving away their books.

A woman sits all morning in an empty room.
She burns beeswax candles and sage.
The rainbow-coloured snake in her spine unfurls
into limitless sky.
A thousand shimmering pale pink rose petals
rearrange themselves geometrically
around a purple core.

The more open her heart the less interested,
less interesting, the newspapers:
Though who can resist, in these days of worry
and unrest, despite these many centuries
of training and reflection, the adrenaline rush
of fingernails and knives?

The Ladies of the Sky Court, their coiled hair
shining in the starry lamplight,
dance their gracious courtly Sky Dance.
The stars flare, incandescent,
from their icy galactic distance.
A fierce whistling through the dark.

We who wish to regain our ancient Wisdom
tread our dancing slippers on polished wood,
not on shavings, we save our *Oohlahlahs*
for the berries and the jelly,
not the blossom. We make the choice.
Gold-flecked veins of Light emergent
amidst the swirl of black.

Hole in the wall

She makes poems out of images and sounds
reverberating vividly into silence.
She carries vegetables home from the market
in a little cloth bag.
The red tomatoes grew from small seeds
in the dark earth into thin air.
She sews yellow curtains and hangs them
in the kitchen window: invisible glass
over a hole in the wall.
Everything that is lives in everything
that is not.

How delicious, how fragrant

She walks to her office each morning
and switches on her computer.
The light in her solar plexus keeps her
from trading on the market of harm.

The students' cello recital sends exquisite
vibrations through the university halls.
Candlelight glints and shimmers through
the cognac and brandy glasses
on the tables of the alumni dinner.

How different the stillness
in her backyard at midnight!
Leaves rustle, stars glitter and fall.
Earth breathes silent fire into the air.
No crickets, no moths, no chickadees sing.

And yet, how lit up the emptiness,
the darkness at the core
of the Tree of Life. How radiant,
how delicious, how fragrant,
for those who know its charm.

The future universe

There, there, among the quivering
viscera, curled in darkness,
the tender pulse of the future universe
breathes in, breathes out,
feel Her quickening,
the first butterfly kicks
of Her royal feet and fists,
yes, even in you, who thought
you were too old or masculinist,
or barren, getting ready to give Birth.

Who can understand

The Spirit enters even where
there are no openings.
Evergreens sway gracefully in the sun.
The mourning dove sends prayers
at sundown over the heaving land.

Morning glory

How can we talk about
the great Cosmic Mother who gave us
Life and being without
distorting and diminishing
Her limitless Beauty and Power?

The Names that can be named
are not Her Name.

Yet we sing:
the Mistress of *Nothing* gave birth
to the billions upon billions upon billions
of creatures on this earth, each with Her kind,
and She takes care of them all.

Her Grandeur is unfathomable.
Her Mystery is deeper and darker
than the darkest Mysteries in all the Galaxies.
She is the Source from whence we came.
She is the very Essence of Life,
the Meaning of All That Is.

Alleluia

The Queen of Heaven is grand,
and gorgeous and sweet-lipped,
and imposing.
She is also wayward, fickle,
promiscuous, of many minds
all at once,
drifting this way and that,
like an unmoored canoe.
The billions upon billions
of stars and planets
and myriad creatures upon them,
duckbilled, flatfooted,
longnecked, spotted, winged,
hairy, hairless, all came from Her,
and She loves them all, completely,
no matter which way they swim,
or walk, or fly, or run,
how quickly or slowly
they light up, and expire.
She rules the galaxies
with a completely open,
completely accepting
heart and hand.
She has completely renounced
Her power to rule
over anything, and yet
in this abdication,
this great, grand, gracious giveaway,
She remains Supreme.
She is all things to all creatures,
everywhere and nowhere.

Fisherwoman

She whose courage
lies in daring, conquers.
She whose courage lies
in daring not to conquer,
offers opportunities
for transformation.
The way of the Great Mother
is not to fight, but to win
anyway, not to pronounce,
yet to call forth deep response,
not to hurry and scurry,
yet to bring everyone home.
She is like a fisherwoman
who waits quietly in her little boat
near Gimli, at the edge of
Lake Winnipeg, at sundown,
saying and doing nothing.
She casts her nets wisely
and at the end of each day
brings home a great catch.
Heaven's nets are like that.
They are wide and strong.
They may be coarsely woven
of rough hemp, but
nothing ever escapes them.

Ladies, ladies

Say what you have to say
and stop talking.
The hurricane blows across the prairies
and it's gone.
The rain pours on the wheat fields,
moves over the skyscrapers
and vanishes.
Let's be like the wind and rain.
Let's pour ourselves out completely
and retreat back into sunlight.
Believe in the people you are talking to,
for they too have inner wisdom,
they too are trying to become wise.

Mandje Mandje Timpe Te

The newly appointed President diminishes
the balled up negative energies
in her departments by offering everyone
more—space.
She undermines the angry
opposing voices in her halls
by—listening to them.
She sidesteps the rebellious
dissenting administrators
by—giving them more say.
She takes away
the motive for mutiny,
giving all their due.
Before we know it
She has us all eating out of her hand!
Sshh! It's the secret
of all real power, and best left
at the bottom of Lake Winnipeg,
with the silver-scaled fishes
who know how to make, and keep,
and give, wishes!

Sturdy hiking boots

She of grace and intelligence
embraces wisdom warmly and eagerly.
As soon as she recognizes the glow
of the Divine before her,
she takes steps to follow.

She of moderate understanding
feels of two minds and—dilly-dallies.
She of coarse mind sees the glow
and laughs.
(If she did not laugh, it would not be
the glow of the Divine!)

The lit up path sometimes seems wayward.
The highway through the mountains
is often strewn with boulders.
Lovely deeds sometimes seem questionable.
Pure white shimmers and is hard to see.
Enough often seems inadequate.
Strong often seems flimsy.
Beautiful often seems plain.

The great Power that animates
all of life is invisible, lacks substance
and fanfare, yet brings all that lives
to its rich, gorgeous ripened fullness.

Teal blue scarves

Even those who lack good sense
ride their bicycles competently and well
on the main path,
as long as it goes straight ahead
with no sudden turnoffs.
Main paths with many people on them
are indeed pleasurable and easy to navigate.
We ride together.

But we humans love side roads.
We spend our pay cheques
and don't think into the future,
or even about next fall, or spring.
We wear the latest fashions, teal blue scarves,
pinstriped trousers, and black heels.
We buy jewellery.
We carry fashion handbags.
We drive fancy cars.
We eat and drink too much.
We wear bling.

So much depends upon

Facing the sun our backs are in the shade.
Breathe in the harmony of both.
No one wants to be orphaned,
or desolate or poor.
Yet great leaders often experience
themselves this way.
Sometimes you become rich
by becoming poor.
Sometimes riches impoverish.
Solitude is better than violence.

I touch the earth,
the earth touches me

Great runners do not rush forward,
they pace themselves and breathe.
Great advocates do not display rage,
they review all sides of the issue
with fairness and calm.
Great leaders lead without controversy.
Great entrepreneurs act graciously.
This is the way talented composers create music.
This is the way meadowlarks sing.
This is the way goldenrod grows in the sun.
This is the way mystics touch Heaven.

Coyotes do not carry her away

She is protected by the purity of her intent
like an innocent baby.
Wasps do not sting her, ravens do not caw
or claw at her,
coyotes do not carry her away.
Her bones are soft, her ligaments weak,
but her hands are strong.

Even without meditation, without ritual,
without strengthening exercise
or ecstatic experience and expression,
she is completely alive and lively,
she is whole.
She breathes in the aroma of the Divine.
In her hot and cold, soft and hard,
light and dark, sweet and savoury
are found in perfect harmony.
She can sing—or laugh—or cry—all day
without getting hoarse.

It is when she fills up her life with too many
attentions that she invites trouble.
She becomes distracted,
her heart begins to feed on itself.
She ages and turns brittle.
Whatever veers from the purity of her intent
leads to death.

Hole in your pocket

Like flies to wanton boys are we to the gods.
A wise teacher too is careless.
To her the students are flimsy presences,
made much of in the moment
then quickly let go.

In us is a huge and generous
store of *Nothing*.
Treasure up the coins of *nothing*
in the pocket of your heart,
your limitless bank account.

Wagging their tails

Great rivers, great seas
rule the earth by finding the lowest,
widest, deepest places.
If you want to lead the people,
find that place of greatest depth
and giving in yourself.

If you want to inspire people,
place yourself behind them.
That's how you can encourage them
without crushing them,
it's how you can guide them
without bringing them to harm.

All we like sheep long to be nudged
and fussed over
by a gentle Shepherdess
who does not compete with us,
does not sweat, nor strive.
We, sheep and Shepherdess,
we are a team.

Shaktipat

She is the Ocean towards which
all streams flow.
She is the Earth in which
all living beings are rooted.
At Her core is the Fire of Creation,
the cradle of poetry and diamonds,
the seedbed of feathers
and blood.

After the rain

People like to give to those who have a lot already,
and turn away from those who have far, far too little.

She who is wise and practices generosity daily
makes offerings of kindness to everyone she meets,

neither in supplication nor pity, but in the grateful
sharing of her inner and outer tenderness and worth.

Our Great Mother is like that. She shines in the gorgeous
multicoloured rainbow that marks the end of the rain.

She casts Her benign Iridescence over the whole Earth,
bending the far reaches of Her limitless Power

in towards the middle, so everyone can enjoy life
in the embrace of Her Divine Bounty and have enough.

Scent of lilacs

If enough people honoured stillness,
everything would be transformed.
Find the calm, creative, golden
emptiness of *Nothing* in yourself,
right here, in the midst of
the world's hurry and bustle.
Stillness can bring you
illumination and joy.
It's impossible to understand
unless you've tasted the sweet
delicious nectar of stillness
in yourself. Scent of lilacs,
Breath of the Divine.

Wild parsley

Only she who is kind can also be brave.
Only she who lives simply can also be generous.
Only she who refuses force is able to reign
with justice. The Great Mother arms
those She favours with kindness.

Divine seed pearl

If the world's leaders carried
even a grain of the Divine seed pearl,
the people would bow in admiration.
The deserts would blossom
and the oceans teem with new life.
There would be no laws or fences,
and yet the people and animals
would dwell in harmony and peace.

To those who aspire to the wisdom
of the Great Harmony everything
will be given simply and naturally.
The way milkweed grows quietly
along ditches and riverbanks,
sustaining monarch butterflies
on their flight, the way jewelweed
offers its balm to passersby
near patches of poison ivy.
Bright flash of blue jays
and yellow finches overhead.

Shade the lamps

Those who know don't say so.
Those who don't know hold forth.
Close the doors,
shutter the windows,
sheath the knives,
untangle the ropes and electrical cords,
shade the lamps, wash the floors.

Find the place inside you
that shines without light,
sparkles without colour,
sings without sound.
Once you find that still Centre
deep within, you can't be
seduced or shocked,
bribed or threatened,
elevated or shamed.

Not so fast, not so much

Fill a bowl to the brim, and it will surely overflow.
Grind your knives to their sharpest point,
and you'll wish you stopped sooner.
If you fill your dresser with diamonds and gold,
how will you keep it secure?
Extreme heroism and achievement
and ostentatious wealth breed disrespect,
and lead to violence and ruin.
Do what you came to do, and withdraw!
That is Heaven's way.

Sorrel soup

The raspberry canes in Her Garden
are deep-rooted.
The hand in Her Hand is secure.
Through Her Grandeur everything
is made new.

Embrace Her Radiance, and your life
shall be enlightened. Invite Her Beauty
into your home and your family
shall enjoy splendour.

> *Raspberry tarts and tea.*
> *Oma's sorrel soup, the consolation*
> *of summery green leaves*
> *in the milky winter broth.*

Bring Her Fragrance into the village
and the community will become sweet-scented
and gentle in its relations. Emulate
Her Strength in the country
and the country will become resilient.

Celebrate Her Generosity to the world,
and the world will become tender-hearted.
Praise Mother, Sun, and Holy Spirit.
Alleluia.

For just as through yourself
you know the Self,
and through your home
you experience Home,

and through your community
you participate in Community,
and through your country
you understand what a Country is,

so through your world, moving from
the inside out, you become the World.
How do I know these things to be true?
She breathes *here*, in me.

Starblanket

Really, why solve problems in such a way
as to create more problems?
She who is wise holds her end of the bargain
but doesn't go after everyone else for the rest.
She who holds the power of wisdom is generous;
she who does not hold wisdom is judgemental.
The way of the Grand-Mother
may seem lowly, and insipid, and trite
against the machinations of worldly power,
but there is such Grace in Her, such foresight,
She keeps the Good perpetually supplied.

Sometimes I feel
like a motherless child

She was there at the beginning
of all things, and also our own beginning.
She is our true Mother.

We know Her, and so we also know
Her many other children.
We never let go of Her hand.

Look inside yourself
to find Her strength.

All around, people are caught up
in power games and getting rich,
or merely staying alive.
That's how they lose their way.

Practice stillness.
Hold onto the thin red thread
that connects the outer to the inner,
that leads us back to the eternal

Maternal Light within.

Jazz festival

Let's get rid of education in manners,
and everyone's grief will end!
Between *thou* and *you*,
what's after all the difference?
"When in Rome, do as the Romans
do" is false advice!

Everyone is dressed up and
ready to celebrate
at the midsummer jazz festival.
Me, I'm sitting at home all alone,
dazed and helpless,
like a baby that's just been born.

In fact I'm more like an idiot,
my brain is completely blank.
Everyone else is eating and drinking,
laughing and singing.
I sit here all alone in the dark,
doing nothing.

I'm restless and confused,
I drift and swirl, my mind wavers
and flickers, this way and that.
Everyone has abandoned me.
I'm such a fool.

But here's the thing: I'm supping
from the Great Mother's breast.

Thorns and brambles

Act on your wish and then stop.
Don't take advantage of the vulnerable.
Where armies live, thorns and brambles grow.
The bigger the army the greater the famine that follows.
Thus is strength followed by decay.
Move only when movement cannot be avoided.
Action as the last resort.

Fried pickerel

Managing the affairs of this world
is like frying that small pickerel you caught
in the early morning hours
on Lake Winnipeg,
just as the sky began to turn pink,
then orange, then golden
in the hushed silence
of the early morning.
The less you poke at it the better.

Centre yourself in the deep core
of Stillness, at the heart of All That Is,
and opposing tendencies will vanish.
Refrain from harming yourself, or others.
This is how you will find comrades
who also seek wisdom and calm.
Invite your neighbour for breakfast.
Serve hot.

Unter den Linden

Like every confident leader
the new CEO gauges her opponents
across the room (the city, the sea)
with precision.
If she's not sure of their strength,
she holds her position
without moving.
If she realizes advancing is not possible,
she strategically retreats
a few steps.

In the glass windowed boardrooms
of her offices, in coffee shops,
in the videotaped streets,
everywhere we see her casually pushing back
the tailored sleeves of her suit jacket
(her hoodie, her silk blouse).
She does not hold out her bare arm.
She enjoys feeling her hand's strength
without a weapon in it,
her mind's clarity and alertness
without a battle to plan.

The greatest of all calamities is to attack
and find there is no enemy.
You end up risking the very thing
you were hoping to protect!
Day by day, she is learning to negotiate
win-win outcomes for everyone.

A tiny winged seed

Make plans long before
the alarm has sounded!
What's soft is easily melted,
what's tender is easily digested.
Create order long before
the state of confusion.

That grand old Poplar tree
on the west bank
of the surging Red River
began as a tiny winged seed.
That new glass and steel
downtown high-rise began
with a handful of dirt.

The travellers who journeyed
all the way around
the world set out with
a few tentative steps.

If you act in haste or panic,
if you grab and shout and stomp
about up to the very last minute,
you may end up damaging
the very thing you cherished most,
and lose the shining treasure
you most wanted to protect.

Let's think about where we're going:
what will be the final result?
The Wise Woman resists
difficult, heroic action.
She values what's gentle,
and soft, and small, and slow.

She points us back to a simpler life
that offers, in the end—
and also all along the way—
more happiness.

Deer in the headlights

She respects good people,
but she also respects bad people—
so they have some good in them!

She believes honest people,
but she also believes liars—
so they have some truth in them!

She seems naive and innocent
in the way she approaches the world,
much like a baby or young child.

She doesn't seem to have a heart
of her own, and often behaves as if
other people's hearts are hers.

Sometimes she looks and acts so
"deer in the headlights"
we laugh at her—and forget to thank her.

For though she lives in a lowly hut
and seems lost amidst the hustle
and bustle of the world,

she is a Wise Woman, and her wisdom
spreads among us like profligate diamonds
scattered on sunlit waves,

inspiring us to reach the higher octave
in our singing, infecting us all with her Spirit
of generosity and shyness and grace.

Taste it

If you want to be a fair guardian
of your country
(garden, home),
take a pinch of dirt
from under your feet
and put it on your tongue.

Only when you have tasted
the literal standing ground
of the people
(vegetables, birds, children)
can you understand
and direct them.

The chickens run loose
in the yard.
The barn swallows flit
and swoop under the eaves.
The cottonwoods flutter
loudly in the breeze.

The graceful trees' heart-
shaped leaves and the crimson
five-pointed cores
in their arching branches
remember their origin
in the stars.

The Grandmothers of Old

The Grandmothers of Old
took great delight in us.
They laid us in skillfully woven
grass blankets and sang
the old songs to us.
They prepared a feast for us
in the land of dearth.
They lifted up our hearts.

> *Schloap, Bebe, schloap,*
> *de Paape heidt de Schoap,*
> *de Maame scheddat det Boumche,*
> *en rauf fällt en Troumche,*
> *schloap, Bebe, schloap.*

Do not "teach" others.
Do not threaten or reward them
or measure how well they listen to you.
Show them your skill and
inspire them to develop
their own different skills.
Challenge them to rise up
to the full height
of their wisdom.

If you can do this truly
you will evoke the power
that can take the world
back to
        the Great Harmony.

Yellow as gold

Look into the middle distance,
soften your eyes.
See the sunlight shining through
the Ash sapling's light
bright new green leaves.

Slow your breath, until it's even
and soft like a child's.
Clear your attention of all distraction,
until you reach the starry core
of silence within you.

The same radiant *Nothing*
in the new leaves
allows them to eat Light.

Can you love the people
around you,
can you nurture and influence
them without controlling
or managing or leaning on them?

Can you serve them lightly,
like a dancer, or a butterfly,
or dandelion in the grass,
delighting, inspiring, feeding them
without fixing them,
and requiring tribute?

Can she bake a cherry pie

When the Ruling Families are desperate,
the press enjoys its heydey.
When the Royals bask in magnificence,
the people feel left out.
The pendulum of favour swings
this way, then that.

There is a place beyond contraries,
where happiness reigns
without depending on another's sadness.
The Oak tree shares its acorns
without withering.
The sun shines on all alike.

The secret to good pie crust
is adding a spoonful of vinegar to the
flour and butter.
Fluff and press into the pan.
Don't overmix.

The Wise Woman influences
without imposing, shapes
without challenging,
nurtures without causing pain.
She invites all the neighbours
to her Royal tea party.

Sour red cherries make the best pie.
Toss the pits in the garden to grow
new seedlings in the spring
for others to enjoy.
Lattice the top crust
so you can see the crimson fruit

bubbling through the crust
when the pie emerges
from the oven, piping hot,
and ready to eat. Serve
with fresh whipped cream
and coffee made from the
dandelion roots in the yard.

Law and order

When we were no longer at peace
we began to speak of duty.
When the country was dark with strife
we began to hear of loyalty and obedience.

We have a secret

New babies are tender
and supple.
Often the old have become
(unnecessarily)
arthritic and brittle.

Emulate the robins
who sing to the morning
and build sweet downy nests
for their young.

See how they brighten up
the grass with
their crimson feathers
and burbling song.

The robins avoid
the harsh winter, but
come back again
in spring,

to the same Elm trees
in the same green-leafy
shaded yard.

Live your life gently.
Sympathy and kindness
are the animating
principles of life,

and make possible
the sweet birth of all
living creatures, each
with her special art.

This is how the meek
inherit the Earth.
Pink and orange petals nod
in the sun.
Sky sparkles.

Quipu

Don't worry if your country
(village, county) is small.
You could organize life so beautifully
that even if you brought in many
technological innovations
and modern conveniences,
cell phones, iPhones, and Android devices,
the people wouldn't use them.

There might be trains and airplanes
and motorcycles and cars,
but the people wouldn't travel.
They would be ready to die
several times over
rather than leave their home locale.

Guns might be available
but the people wouldn't be interested
in owning or using them.
There might be paper, and books,
and pens, and laptops,
but they would be left untouched.

You could make it so your people,
truly, wouldn't want or need anything
for writing except knotted string!
Without the distractions and excesses
of television, newspapers, and the internet,
the people would focus on enjoying
their lives together as simply
and elegantly as possible.

They would catch goldeye and pickerel,
gather blackberries,
and grow carrots and beets
and marigolds in their small gardens.
They would weave their own linens,
and wash them by hand.
They would build their own cottages
(tipis, yurts), and tend their few
horses, and plum trees, and goats.
They would sew their own shoes.

The next country (village, county)
might be so close by you could hear
radios blaring, cars honking,
and dogs barking,
but the people would prefer walking
in their neighbourhoods,
enjoying the purple and gold sunset
with their handful of friends.
They would live and die
without ever having been there.

There is a crack in everything

The most perfect bowl is flawed,
yet holds water.
The labour that went into
creating the greatest dances
becomes invisible.
The quickest way home
often seems roundabout.

The most skillful mode is approximate.
Eloquent words stammer.
Moving around, stamping your feet,
assuages cold.
But sitting quietly, conserving energy,
overcomes heat.
So much depends upon.

No matter what the event
(action, thing) connecting
the moving parts to the Whole,
or outcomes to their Source,
She puts everything right
under Heaven.

White coral bells

Overstimulation of the senses
makes people dull,
and bored, and boring.
Bright lights, loud sounds,
exotic tastes weary quickly.
Then we need more
and more and more
and more and more.
Luxury items, fast cars,
expensive felt hats, exotic
leather shoes come
with the weight of their
cosmopolitan provenance.
Constant competition
drives people insane.
The Wise Woman avoids
depleting her Spirit with
overstimulation of the senses,
acquisitiveness
and overachievement,
and chooses instead
simplicity, local enjoyments,
Lily of the valley 'neath
the garden walk.
She values good digestion,
inner radiance, and
quiet joy.

Old woman

She gathers sticks in an abandoned yard
to burn in her rustic wood stove.
She hums a lullaby for her faraway children.
Her breasts sag with the memory
of eager lips and sweet milk.

She is like the Manitoba Maple tree
leaning over the swollen Assiniboine River,
which senses its own nearing reflection
in the rushing water. And holds firm.

She is like the Siberian Elm tree,
exuberant in prairie sunlight,
waving its ten thousand branches
despite high wind, profusely
in the gold-flecked air.

Arctic dream

Her Womb is empty yet sustains
the World without ever being depleted.
Her embrace is infinite, without end.
She is the Cosmic Grand-Mother
of All That Lives.

Her song is sweet,
Her wisdom is subtle.
Her love is fierce, and limitless.

She is like the great Ocean
that cradles the Earth,
the Darkness in the bulging
middle of the Milky Way.
We cannot see Her all at once.

Did She too have a Mother?
No one knows.
We know She was there before
the First Breath, the First Element,
the First Sound.

Basic arithmetic

The people don't really fear death.
In any case, the Goddesses of Destruction
are always on standby, ready to serve
with pestilence and plague,
lightning and earthquake.
Families and governments teeter
perpetually on the brink of
disagreement, feuding, war.
Let's not scare the people
with death or the threat of death.
They know famine is caused by
human injustice, not from parsimony
or caprice in our Mother,
who steadily offers all Her children
opportunity and plenitude.
There is already much death
and threat of death in the world.
Let's not add to it!

White stork spreads wings

You could live so that you no longer carry
death and the fear of death in you.
If you met a wild moose
or a cougar, you would not be harmed.
Bison, bears, and mountain goats
would find no weak spots to claw at
or trample or gore in you.
You could walk through the fields of war
and remain untouched by bullets
and bombs whizzing through the air.
Your life would flourish
without effort or strife.
You would have released death
and the fear of death in you.

Sweet Georgia Brown

Coming *home*,
that weak trembly shaky feeling
inside your bones.
This is the only important,
the only real, thing.

Stalwart protectors of the Deep

Most living beings have not forgotten
the generosity and power of the Grand-Mother.
They honour their relations with one another,
they keep their part in preserving the Great Harmony.
The deep blue Sky remains
translucent and calm.
The round blue green Earth
holds her precise place and motion
intact in the turning Galaxy.
Oak trees and cherry blossoms,
foxes and cows, and songbirds
and humans,
each preserve their form.
The mothers (and sometimes fathers
and others) take tender care
of the young.
The great Oceans remain
stalwart protectors of the Deep.
Presidents and Prime Ministers and Queens
direct their people to get along
and practice reciprocity
in their negotiations and transactions.
The world over people sing and dance
and tell stories together.
None of this could happen without
the sweet harmonious oversight
of the Great Mother, in whose
humming, cradling, spinning, singing
embrace we are held.

For without translucence,
the Sky would rip and shred.
Without precision and steadiness,
the Earth would wobble
and spin out of control.
Without the stalwart protection
of the Oceans, the Deep
would get clogged and dry up.
Without the care and kindness
of all living species towards their young,
Life on Earth would cease.
Without considerable wisdom and honour
in their government of the people,
Prime Ministers and Queens
would immediately be overthrown.
All the sympathetic resonances
of Earth and Heaven are part
of the Great Harmony.
Let's proceed with humility,
remembering our small part in
preserving the shimmering, vibrating,
live, breathing network of
the Great Whole.

Can you do it

Pursuing knowledge means filling up
your library and filing cabinets
and bookshelves, and buying more
pens and notebooks and dictionaries.

Pursuing wisdom means subtracting
activities, and accomplishments,
and belongings,
until you get to stillness.

This is where everything can be renewed
and transformed
without interference or strife,
sitting alone in deep Silence.

Consider the lilies

The Wise Woman knows how to
accomplish difficult challenges
in easy simple ways,
while they are still small.
But many easy accomplishments
still add up to considerable difficulty.
So the Wise Woman has learned
how to make the easy difficult
and so avoids difficulty altogether!

The way of water

Water nourishes the ten thousand creatures
and likes best the lowest places
that others reject.
The Wise Woman, too, builds her house
on humble, simple ground.

Each time she chooses to invest
in clear thinking, gentle friends,
truthful words, effective action,
she is choosing the way
                    of water.

Wave hands like clouds

Knowing you don't know
is the beginning of Wisdom.
Thinking you know
when you really don't
is a big problem! It's a sickness!

Recognizing this problem,
this sickness, in your own mental
and emotional habits
is the beginning of the cure.

Recognize yourself as sick
and become well!

Divine Kindergarten

If we stopped looking
for strong leaders
or saintly figures
to lead and overshadow us,
if we stopped advertising
skillful feats and luxury items
only a few can afford,
jealousy and stealing
would end.

We could make it so
everyone would be
well-practiced in the arts
of cooking, archery, singing,
building, and making pots.
We are all children in Her
capacious Divine
Kindergarten, offered
limitless opportunities
to learn the practical
and ornamental skills
of the good life
through the gentle
sharing of curiosity,
imagination, and free play.

Shadows and shapes

We cannot see Her.
We cannot hear Her.
We cannot feel Her Touch.
Her Presence is Invisible.
Looking for Her
we encounter many Unnameable
shadows and shapes.

Yet we can know Her.
We can hold Her Hand.
We can intuit Her Wisdom.
We can feel Her Essence,
recognize Her Might.

Hold on to the red thread
that can bring you back
from wandering
to Her Love, Her Grandeur,
Her Light.

Spindly burled trunks

She sits in her little room
looking out onto sparkling snow.
The fire crackles in the stove.

The smouldering wood seethes
and hisses, dropping sparks
into the ash below.

She cries out for consolation
to the bright Moon
shining through the window

in the deepening silence,
the bustling world receding
from her view.

She looks inward, and sees
Black Quartz glinting
in her breast.

Sitting alone like this,
curled around her sorrow,
letting herself become

gnarled and twisted,
like the stunted Maple trees
along the Red River

with their spindly burled trunks
acquired in rough weather,
tracing her way carefully

back through her suffering
to golden Stillness, this is how
she becomes Whole.

Ojo Caliente

The Poet surveys the world
on eagle wings,
circling around and around
from the outside in.

She settles gently
into the red brown arms of
the Siberian cherry tree
in her garden, in full moonlight,
in the blue snow.
Silence.

This day she travels down, down
through the pungent rot of darkness
to the glittering underground
Black Diamond River winding
through its floor.

A grass woven dragon boat
awaits to ferry her along the
reedy shore to a wooden palace.
Slowly the weathered doors
open to let her in.
Come, the Royals in their
embroidered finery beckon, come.

A sunbeaten wrinkled smiling woman
in a beaded headdress offers her
a wooden bowl filled with light
to take back up to share
with the suffering air.

Another day she is swept up
up, up into ice covered mountains
to bring a human lullaby
to the grassy nest of crystal-headed
baby eaglets hatching out
our as yet unimagined future there.

She walks among us

She wears a rough skirt
but carries rare pearls in Her pockets.
Her words are easy to understand
but the people do not listen.
They do not hear Her Royal accent.

Greensleeves

She who is wise accomplishes her task
and withdraws.
And then everyone says,
isn't that amazing,
it happened all by itself!

Acknowledgements

The poetic epigraphs on page vii are from Li Bai (Li Bo)'s lyric poem "Song of the Transcendent Person Jade Verity," collected in the *Ch'üan Tang shih* (Taipei: Fu hsing Bookstore, 1967, 948), translated into English by Suzanne E. Cahill in Cahill's *Transcendence and Divine Passion: The Queen Mother of the West in Medieval China* (Stanford: Stanford University Press, 1993, 217); and Louise Bernice Halfe's *Blue Marrow* (Regina: Coteau Books, 2004, 97). They appear here with the permission of their respective publishers. The epigraph by Julian of Norwich is from Grace Warrack's translation of *Revelations of Divine Love* ("Chapter LX" and "Chapter LXI." London: Methuen & Company, 1901. http://www.gutenberg.org/files/52958/52958-h/52958-h.htm).

Robert Majzels' inspired term "trans*inha*lation" can be found in his essay on creative re-translations of ancient texts, "*Sì èr bù sì*: Translating Translating 85," published in *Translating Translating Montréal: words on translation/works through translation* by Oana Avasilichioaei, Angela Carr, Robert Majzels, and Erín Mouré (Montreal: pressdust/University of Calgary, 2007, 29-34). Luce Irigaray's notion of "placental logic," and the generosity of the womb and maternal body in engendering and nurturing male and female infants alike, can be found in her monograph *je, tu, nous: Toward a Culture of Difference*, translated by Alison Martin (New York and London: Routledge, 1993). First Nations figures of the Divine Feminine and Indigenous cosmologies are outlined in Keres poet and knowledge keeper Paula Gunn Allen's inspiring compilation, *Grandmothers of the Light: A Medicine Woman's*

Sourcebook (Boston: Beacon Press, 1991). Her observations about the misogynist aims of European colonial conquest of the Americas appear in the section, "The Ways of Our Grandmothers," in her outstanding study, *The Sacred Hoop: Recovering the Feminine in American Indian Traditions* (Boston: Beacon Press, 1986, 9-50). Adrienne Rich's resonant phrase "of woman born" (borrowed from the witches' misleading prophecy to Macbeth in Shakespeare's famous play by that name) was also the title of her groundbreaking book on maternal thinking, *Of Woman Born: Motherhood as Experience and Institution* (W.W. Norton, 1976; Bantam, 1977; Virago, 1979, 1986). Louis Komjathy traces the Daoist precept to become "inwardly still and outwardly reverent" to the ancient teaching text, the Guanzi, or Book of Master Guan, translated by Komjathy in Vol. 1 of a 10-volume series, *Handbooks for Daoist Practice and Inward Training* (2003; repr., Hong Kong: Yuen Yuen Institution, 2008).

The following English translations of Laozi's *Dao De Jing* were particularly helpful in my own poetic meditations and re-translations, among others: Ellen M. Chen's *The Tao Te Ching: A New Translation with Commentary* (St. Paul: Paragon House, 1989); Chichung Huang's *Tao Te Ching: A Literal Translation* (Fremont: Asian Humanities Press, 2003); DC Lau's *Tao Te Ching* (New York: Penguin Classics, 1964); Stephen Mitchell's *Tao Te Ching: A New English Version* (New York: HarperCollins, 1988); and Arthur Waley's *Tao Te Ching* with Introduction by Robert Wilkinson (Hertfordshire: Wordsworth, 1997). I am indebted to the following scholarly works about the *Dao De Jing* and the Daoist contemplative heritage and legacy, among many others: Suzanne E. Cahill's *Transcendence and Divine Passion: The Queen Mother of the West in Medieval China* (Stanford: Stanford University Press, 1993); Thomas Cleary's *Immortal Sisters: Secret Teachings of Taoist Women* (1989; repr., Berkley: North Atlantic Books, 1996); JJ Clarke's *The Tao of the West: Western Transformations of Taoist Thought* (London and New York: Routledge, 2000); Catherine Despeux and Livia Kohn's *Women in Daosim* (Cambridge: Three Pines Press, 2003); Livia Kohn's *God of the Dao: Lord Lao in History and Myth* (Ann Arbor: University of Michigan Center for Chinese Studies, 2000), *Early Chinese Mysticism: Philosophy and Soteriology in the Taoist Tradition* (Princeton: Princeton University Press, 1992), *Pristine Affluence: Daoist Roots in the Stone Age* (St. Petersburg: Three Pines Press, 2017), and *The Taoist Experience: An Anthology* (Albany: State University of New York Press, 1993); Louis Komjathy's *Daoism: A Guide for the Perplexed* (London and New York: Bloomsbury, 2014); Thomas Michael's *The Pristine Dao: Metaphysics in Early Daoist Discourse* (Albany: SUNY Press, 2005); and Isabelle Robinet's *Taoist Meditation: The Mao-shan Tradition of Great Purity*, translated by Julian F. Pas and Norman J. Girardot (Albany: SUNY Press, 1993), from the French *Méditation taoïste* (Paris: Dervy Livres, 1979).

Poetic and scholarly influences on the poetics side of the project are too many to list here; let me mention just a few relevant recent essays: Neal Alexander's 2016 essay "Place, locality, and late modernist poetry," on locality in modern English poetry and the relationship between traditional *genius loci* and the Divine Feminine (lecture,

Vibrant Localism conference, University of Exeter, Devon, June 24, 2016, http://www.academia.edu/26538055/ Place_locality_and_late_modernist_poetry); Xiaosheng Yang's literary critical dissertation, "A Daoist Perspective on George Oppen's Poetry and Poetics" (PhD diss.,University of Alabama, 2016, http://acumen.lib.ua.edu/content/ u0015/0000001/0002237/u0015_0000001_0002237.pdf); and John Z. Ming Chen and Yuhua Ji's *Canadian-Daoist Poetics, Ethics, and Aesthetics: An Interdisciplinary and Cross-cultural Study*, which presents an interesting survey of Canadian literary writing influenced by Daoism (Berlin and Heidelberg: Springer-Verlag, 2016).

The poems contain numerous whimsical and passing references to cultural intertexts of my own surround. I cite the most obvious of them here: "Ishtar, fish star" quotes the dedication to Canadian poet Phyllis Webb's *Naked Poems* (Vancouver: Periwinkle Press, 1965). "Spider Grandmother" references the originary Creatrix in Keres creation myth (*Grandmothers of the Light*, 33-37). The "Great Mother" recalls Divine Feminine figures of worship from around the world: for a global overview, see Barbara Mor and Monica Sjöö's *The Great Cosmic Mother: Rediscovering the Religion of the Earth* (San Francisco: Harper & Row, 1987), one among many available such studies; in Daoist cosmology, She is venerated as the Mother of the Dao, who gives birth to Lord Lao, known as Laozi in his human form, and worshipped in His Divine form as the Supremely Mysterious and Primordial Emperor (Chap. 1-2 in *Women in Daoism*). She is also more widely known (in another incarnation) as *Xiwangmu*, Queen Mother of the West, or the Greatly Numinous and Ninefold Radiant Mother of Metal of Tortoise Ter-race, or the Ninefold Numinous and Greatly Wondrous Mother of Metal of Tortoise Mountain (*The Taoist Experi-ence*, 55-62). *Oma* is German for "Grandmother" or "Grandma." "Queen of Heaven" in Mediterranean tradi-tion can refer to Ishtar, Babylonian goddess of Creation; Asherah, Sumerian queen consort of the god Anu; or Mary, the Mother of Jesus. "Angel-covered Ark" echoes the description of the cherubim-covered gold chest of ancient Israel, containing sacred articles in the *Book of Exodus*. "Your exquisite Dance of Veils" recalls the sacred, life-enhancing, ceremonial women's veil dance of Middle Eastern tradition, dating back to ancient Babylonian and Hebrew times, in the worship of Ishtar and Inanna, and often danced in support of women's childbirth labour as outlined in Toni Bentley, *Sisters of Salomé* (Lincoln: Uni-versity of Nebraska Press, 2005, 30-36); the dance became associated, centuries later, with the perverse, murderous dance of Salomé before King Herod II (Matthew 14), and later still with the hypersexualized, orientalized dancer in Oscar Wilde's "decadent" French play *Salomé* (1891); the intent here is to remember the more dignified, originary Goddess-linked Creation-honouring meaning of the Dance. The "Ladies of the Sky Court" recall the visionary experiences of ancient Daoist mystics, who sometimes consorted with goddesses appearing to them in human form (Chap. 1 in *Women in Daoism*). "Alleluia" is a liturgi-cal chant of praise to the Divine in the Jewish and Chris-tian traditions. "*Mandje Mandje Timpe Te*" is part of the summons of the magic flounder who can grant wishes in the folktale "Von dem Fischer un syner Fru," ("The

Fisherman's Wife"), collected by the painter Philipp Otto Runge in Plautdietsch and published in slightly different versions by Achim von Arnim and Clemens Brentano, in their three volume collection of folk poetry *Des Knaben Wunderhorn* (1805, 1808), and later in German by Jacob and Wilhelm Grimm in their collection of *Kinder- und Hausmärchen* (1812), first translated into English by Margaret Hunt in 1884. "So much depends upon" is the first line of William Carlos Williams' lyric poem, "The Red Wheelbarrow." "*I touch the earth,/the earth touches me*" is the opening of the Buddhist slow walking meditation mantra. "Like flies to wanton boys are we to the gods" is from William Shakespeare's play *King Lear*—these words are spoken by Gloucester, slowly awakening to the true nature of the people in his life, after enduring torture and maiming for having shown kindness to his friend, the former King; the next line is "They kill us for their sport" (IV.1.36-37). "Wagging their tails" is a line from the Daoist-like English children's rhyme, "Little Bo Peep/Has lost her sheep/And doesn't know where/To find them,/Leave them alone,/And they will come home,/Wagging their tails/Behind them. "All we like sheep … long for a gentle Shepherdess" echoes the ancient prophetic lament "All we like sheep have gone astray" from Isaiah 53:6, and is the name of a famous chorus in George Frideric Handel's *Messiah*. "The gentle Shepherdess" echoes Psalm 23:1, "The Lord is my Shepherd; I shall not want." "Nothing" recalls Cordelia's refusal to play Lear's game of flattery and favouritism earlier in the play, replying to his request for public homage with the word "Nothing," whereupon Lear angrily and arrogantly and erroneously replies, "Nothing will come of nothing " (1.1.90). The play echoes and ultimately discredits ancient Greek philosopher Parmenides and his followers, who argued, contrary to the creation stories of most religious traditions, including Daoism, that Something could not have come from Nothing. "*Shaktipat*" is a Hindu Sanskrit term for the transmission of spiritual energy through a sacred word or mantra, or by a look, thought or touch, by an act of grace. "Praise Mother, Sun, and Holy Spirit" is a feminized version of the Christian Doxology. "Starblanket" refers to a quilted blanket featuring a five-pointed star (representing the Morning Star), associated with protection and honouring in Indigenous gift-giving ceremonies. "*Sometimes I feel/like a motherless child*" is the first line of a traditional African-American Spiritual, which gives eloquent expression to the anguish of children separated from their families in the American South during the era of slavery. "*Unter den Linden*" is the name of a famous boulevard in Berlin, and the title of a collection of short stories by Berlin author Christa Wolf (1999; repr., Munich: Luchterhand, 2002); the linden tree was held to be sacred in many mythologies of origin, including Slavic, German, and Mediterranean, and ceremonies and political meetings were traditionally held in its shade to promote peace and prosperity. "They prepared a feast for us" echoes Psalm 23:5, "Thou preparest a table before me/in the presence of mine enemies." "*Schloap, Bebe, schloap*" is the first line of a traditional northern European lullaby, in Plautdietsch ("Sleep, baby, sleep" in English, "*Schlaf, Kindlein, schlaf*" in German). "Yellow as gold" recalls the first line of the children's song: "O Dandelion, yellow as gold,/What do you do all day?"

"*Can she bake a cherry pie*" is the first line of an English folksong. "*We have a secret*" is the first line of an English children's rhyme involving a child, a robin, and a "sweet cherry tree." "This is how the meek/inherit the earth" recalls the Daoist-like third teaching in Jesus's famed Sermon on the Mount (Matthew 5:5). "*Quipu*" refers to the traditional record-keeping system of the Inca people, which used knotted strings to code complex messages, now understood to have been written in a binary code similar to that of modern computers. "There is a crack in everything" evokes Leonard Cohen's famous observation about "how the light gets in" in his song "Anthem," released in the audio-recording *Leonard Cohen: The Future,* by SONY in 1992; variations of this line have been credited to Rumi, Ralph Waldo Emerson, and Ernest Hemingway, among others. "*White coral bells*" is the beginning of a traditional English round song for children, with these later lines "Lily of the valley/'neath the garden walk." "*White stork spreads wings*" is the name of a Tai Chi movement. "*Sweet Georgia Brown*" is the name of a jazz standard composed by Ben Bernie and Maceo Pinkard, with lyrics by Kenneth Casey, first released by Ben Bernie and his Hotel Roosevelt Orchestra in 1925. "*Consider the lilies*" is the beginning of a Daoist-like teaching by Jesus in the Gospels, to relax and focus on the coming Kingdom of Heaven rather than getting too caught up in daily cares and worries (Matthew 6:25-34, Luke 12:22-32). "*Wave hands like clouds*" is the name of a Tai Chi movement. "*Ojo Caliente*" means "hot eyes," and is the name of a famous hot springs outside of Santa Fe, New Mexico, said traditionally to hold magical powers. "*Greensleeves*" is the name of a traditional English folksong, often sung at Christmastime. While I have tried to exhaustively acknowledge and correctly cite my influences and inspirations for *Glitter & fall*, I am only human. If an error has been made, please contact Turnstone Press.

The sequence of poems featured in *Glitter & fall* does not replicate the classic sequence of poems in Laozi's *Dao De Jing*, but rather, reflects the process of my poetic engagement with the text and gradual understanding of its precepts in our contemporary intercultural context. Nor is there an exact relationship between my trans*inha*lations and Laozi's poems, though discerning readers of the *Dao De Jing* (if so inclined) may find numerous identifiable correspondences. I give an approximate numerical index here. Note that some of Laozi's poems are reflected more or less obliquely in two or three different trans*inha*lations, while others are absent—the selection process was intuitive: Wild rose petals [49], Ishtar, fish star [25], Rough tongue [6], Highbush cranberry [38], Hole in the wall [13], How delicious, how fragrant [35], The future universe [6], Who can understand [43], Morning glory [1], Alleluia [34], Fisherwoman [73], Ladies, ladies [23], *Mandje Mandje Timpe Te* [15], Sturdy hiking boots [41], Teal blue scarves [53], So much depends upon [42], *I touch the earth,/the earth touches me* [68], Coyotes do not carry her away [55], Hole in your pocket [5], Wagging their tails [66], *Shaktipat* [6], After the rain [77], Scent of lilacs [31], Wild parsley [67], Divine seed pearl [32], Shade the lamps [56], Not so fast, not so much [9], Sorrel soup [54], Starblanket [35], *Sometimes I feel/like a motherless child* [52], Jazz festival [20], Thorns and brambles [30], Fried pickerel [60], *Unter den Linden* [69], A tiny winged seed [64], Deer in the headlights [49], Taste it [78],The Grand-mothers of Old [65], Yellow as gold [10], *Can she bake a cherry pie* [58], Law and order[18], *We have a secret* [76], *Quipu* [80],There is a crack in everything [45], *White coral bells* [12], Old woman [47], Arctic dream [4], Basic arith-metic [74- 75], *White stork spreads wings* [50], *Sweet Geor-gia Brown* [40], Stalwart protectors of the Deep [39], Can you do it [48], *Consider the lilies* [63], The way of water [8], *Wave hands like clouds* [71], Divine Kindergarten [3], Shadows and shapes [14], Spindly burled trunks [22], *Ojo Caliente* [np], She walks among us [70], *Greensleeves* [17].

I thank Han Ququn of Nanjing University, China, for gifting me a few years ago with Arthur Waley's English translation of the *Tao Te Ching,* with the original Chinese text included in Mandarin, which initiated this whole project; Kenneth Nichols of Brandon, Manitoba, for his encouragement, and friendship, and lovely musical set-ting of several of the poems in a suite for soprano, clar-inet, and harp, *Coyotes do not carry her away* premiered by the Brandon Chamber Players in Brandon, Manitoba, in 2013; and Lin Xu for her exquisite ink drawings which became part of a limited edition poetry/art chapbook of earlier versions of the poems, *SHE: Poems inspired by Laozi's Dao De Jing* (Brandon: Radish Press, 2012). Some of the poems appeared previously in *Prairie Fire*'s special issue in honour of Turnstone Press (2017), *Rampike*'s final issue (2014), and *Algoma Ink*'s special issue in memory of Alanna Bondar (2014). Many thanks to Jamis Paulson, Sharon Caseburg, Sarah Ens, and Melissa McIvor for their fine work in turning the manuscript into a beautiful book

Acknowledgements

and sharing it with the world; and to Joanne Arnott for perceptive editorial advice and conversation.

Thank you to the gracious hospitality and teachings of First Nations colleagues, mentors and friends on Turtle Island, whose creative weaving together of traditional and contemporary spiritual and cultural practices, and generosity in sharing their wisdom with newcomers like me, inspired me to pursue a more Feminine-centred vision and relationship to the creative and enabling world of Spirit, Language, Land, and Cosmos. Thank you to my Teachers in several Spiritual Traditions, whose inner radiance and precise care over many years gave me a glimpse of the Great Harmony and introduced me to the generative and transformational presence of what Laozi calls the *Dao*, the great *Nothing*, whose names of manifestation and imagining include the Great Cosmic Grand-Mother of All That Is.

Xiè, xie. Dòjeh. Thank you. *Dankschein. Miigwech. Philamayaye. Marsee.*